*NIJ*

# 2002

# Annual Report

**U.S. Department of Justice
Office of Justice Programs**

810 Seventh Street, N.W.
Washington, DC 20531

**John Ashcroft**
*Attorney General*

**Deborah J. Daniels**
*Assistant Attorney General*

**Sarah V. Hart**
*Director, National Institute of Justice*

This and other publications and products of the
National Institute of Justice can be found
on the World Wide Web at:

**Office of Justice Programs
National Institute of Justice**
*http://www.ojp.usdoj.gov/nij*

# Table of Contents

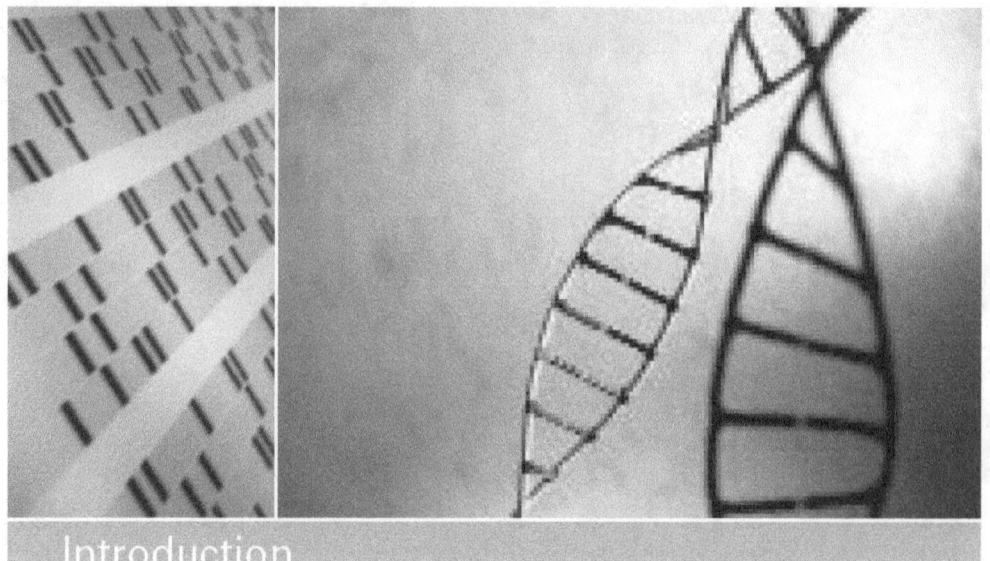

Introduction

# Introduction

As the Department of Justice's research, development, and evaluation agency, NIJ has always been a reliable source of the latest knowledge on criminal justice. In 2002, NIJ developed seven agency-wide strategic goals in three main areas: (1) creating knowledge and tools, (2) disseminating information, and (3) managing the agency's programs. The seven goals are:

◻ Partner with State and local practitioners and policymakers to identify social science research and technology needs.

◻ Create scientific, relevant, and reliable knowledge—with a particular emphasis on terrorism, violent crime, drugs and crime, cost-effectiveness, and community-based efforts—to enhance the administration of justice and public safety.

◻ Develop affordable and effective tools and technologies to enhance the administration of justice.

◻ Disseminate relevant knowledge and information in an understandable, timely, and concise manner.

◻ Act as an honest broker to identify the information, tools, and technologies that respond to the needs of stakeholders.

◻ Practice fairness and openness in the research and development process.

◻ Ensure professionalism, excellence, accountability, cost-effectiveness, and integrity in the management and conduct of NIJ activities and programs.

In addition to these strategic goals, NIJ identified 10 high-priority subject areas: law enforcement and policing; justice systems (sentencing, courts, prosecution, and defense); corrections; investigative and forensic sciences (including DNA); counterterrorism and critical incidents; crime prevention and causes of crime; violence and victimization (including violent crimes); drugs, alcohol, and crime; interoperability, spatial information, and automated systems; and program evaluation.

These priority subject areas and strategic goals will help shape decisions about the scope of future work and the dissemination of NIJ-sponsored research, information, and technologies. At the same time, NIJ will maintain the flexibility to respond to emerging needs and to consider the merits of individual projects that may contribute to other worthwhile goals.

In 2002, NIJ also bolstered its commitment to program evaluation. The Bureau of Justice Assistance and the Office of Juvenile Justice and Delinquency Prevention, sister agencies under the Office of Justice Programs, each developed an evaluation partnership with NIJ and transferred funds totaling $5.3 million and $5.8 million respectively for NIJ to design and procure outcome evaluations. The evaluations will help measure successes in programs, pinpoint shortcomings, and inform future efforts to develop similar programs.

NIJ redesigned its print and electronic products in 2002 as part of an intensified effort to make the knowledge it creates as relevant as possible to policymakers and practitioners. The redesign resulted in a format that emphasizes clear and concise writing with findings and implications stated up front. The redesign helps ensure that research is presented for targeted audiences in a user-friendly format.

NIJ will continue to provide objective, independent, evidence-based knowledge and tools to enhance the administration of justice and public safety. Its reorganization helps achieve this mission.

Highlights of the Year

# Responding to Terrorism

As a result of the terrorist attacks of September 2001 and the subsequent national and international battle against terrorism, NIJ expanded its focus on and capacity to perform research on terrorism. For example, terrorism was added as a specific category in the solicitation for investigator-initiated research in 2002. Plans for a directed solicitation on terrorism research were developed for 2003 funding. This section describes NIJ activities during 2002 that helped the Nation's public safety institutions be better prepared and equipped to respond to a terrorist incident and to investigate terrorist planning and activity.

## Research on how terrorist organizations fund themselves

An effective strategy for combating terrorist networks is to choke off their funding stream. Criminal organizations are often supported by systems or networks of people who transfer money and other resources outside the conventional, regulated financial institutions. These unregulated methods of exchanging money and other commodities are called Informal Value Transfer Systems. Although not necessarily illegal, they have come under scrutiny because they are used by criminal enterprises, including terrorist networks. The Treasury Department's Financial Crimes Enforcement Network (FinCEN) funded a study of Informal Value Transfer Systems to fully understand their mechanisms in this country and to construct effective intervention policies. NIJ partnered with FinCEN to examine the international context in which these unregulated value transfer systems develop and the experiences of other nations that have long confronted them. Also in 2002, at the request of officials from Customs, the FBI, and FinCEN, the research was expanded to develop methods for identifying suspicious trade diversion transactions so that Federal, State, and local regulatory and enforcement agencies can better target and disrupt terrorist financial transfers.

## Workshops on local law enforcement preparedness for terrorism

Local law enforcement plays a critical role in preparing for and responding to terrorism. Local law enforcement officials must confront new demands placed upon them in their efforts to effectively deal with the terrorist threat in their jurisdictions. To assist local law enforcement in this effort, NIJ worked with the Office of Community Oriented Policing Services (COPS) on a series of six workshops on policing and terrorism. Each had a hands-on component developed by COPS and a research component developed by NIJ. The titles of the six workshops were:

- Improving Federal/Local Partnerships.
- Technology and Information Sharing.
- Intelligence Gathering and Analysis.
- Policing Muslim and Arab Communities.

3

□ Community Policing and Terrorism.

□ Local Law Enforcement Preparation for and Response to Terrorist Incidents.

The research component featured leading policing and other relevant researchers who identified information gaps that could be addressed in future NIJ-sponsored studies. The workshops helped NIJ develop a terrorism research agenda that will support local law enforcement agencies in their efforts to effectively counter the terrorist threat.

### Helping to assess chemical facility vulnerability

Facilities that comprise the Nation's infrastructure are potential terrorist targets and must be protected. NIJ released a special report in 2002 providing an overview of a method to assess the security of chemical facilities within the United States. The methodology identifies and assesses potential security threats, risks, and vulnerabilities. It also guides the chemical facility industry in making security improvements.

NIJ developed the vulnerability assessment methodology in collaboration with the Department of Energy's Sandia National Laboratories, which has developed vulnerability assessment methodologies for other critical infrastructure components, including dams, water treatment and supply facilities, correctional facilities, and nuclear facilities.

*The men and women who first respond to the scene of a terrorist attack or other critical incident face a multitude of dangers. It is crucial that first responders be properly equipped.*

**For more information:**

□ *A Method to Assess the Vulnerability of U.S. Chemical Facilities,* Washington, DC: U.S. Department of Justice, National Institute of Justice, November 2002 (NCJ 195171), http://www.ojp.usdoj. gov/nij/pubs-sum/195171.htm.

### Assessing first responder equipment

The men and women who first respond to the scene of a terrorist attack or other critical incident face a multitude of dangers. It is crucial that first responders be properly equipped. In the immediate aftermath of the terrorist attacks of September 11, NIJ rushed to publication a series of draft guides for first responder equipment. These guides provide key information for agencies to consider when purchasing such equipment. During 2002, these publications were among the most requested in NIJ's inventory, in both print and online formats.

**Personal protection equipment.** This NIJ Guide discusses duration of protection; dexterity, mobility, and launderability; and the use and/or reuse of respiratory protection equipment, protective garments, and other protective apparel, including boots, gloves, hoods, and lab coats.

**Communication equipment.** This NIJ Guide provides information on communication equipment for use with chemical and biological protective clothing and respiratory equipment. It presents an overview of communications systems, discusses equipment characteristics and performance parameters, and lists manufacturer-supplied details for 181 specific items.

**Biological agent detection equipment.** This guide identifies the four most common classes of biological agents, discusses the challenges in detecting biological agents, describes detection system components and technologies, and outlines how to prepare for a biological incident.

**Chemical and biological decontamination equipment.** This guide provides information on decontamination equipment for chemical agents, biological agents, and toxic industrial materials. A survey of decontamination equipment known to the authors is included. Brief technical discussions outline the principles for operating such equipment effectively.

**For more information:**

- *Guide for the Selection of Personal Protection Equipment for Emergency First Responders, NIJ Guide 102–00,* Washington, DC: U.S. Department of Justice, National Institute of Justice, November 2002 (NCJ 191518), http://www.ojp.usdoj.gov/nij/pubs-sum/191518.htm.

- *Guide for the Selection of Communication Equipment for Emergency First Responders, NIJ Guide 104–00,* Washington, DC: U.S. Department of Justice, National Institute of Justice, February 2002 (NCJ 191160), http://www.ojp.usdoj.gov/nij/pubs-sum/191160.htm.

- *An Introduction to Biological Agent Detection Equipment for Emergency First Responders, NIJ Guide 101–00,* Washington, DC: U.S. Department of Justice, National Institute of Justice, December 2001 (NCJ 190747), http://www.ojp.usdoj.gov/nij/pubs-sum/190747.htm.

- *Guide for the Selection of Chemical and Biological Decontamination Equipment for Emergency First Responders, NIJ Guide 103–00,* Washington, DC: U.S. Department of Justice, National Institute of Justice, October 2001 (NCJ 189724), http://www.ojp.usdoj.gov/nij/pubs-sum/189724.htm.

## Detecting bombs

NIJ continued its work developing and assessing equipment used for detecting and removing bombs. The Bomb Technician Personal Digital Assistant puts a wealth of information literally into the hands of a bomb technician at an incident. Quick access to numerous manuals, charts, and publications in a wireless palm-sized device gives bomb technicians an edge in performing their dangerous tasks more safely and effectively. NIJ oversaw the development of a prototype device that was used by Fairfax County, Virginia, bomb squad technicians in their role as part of the security contingent at the 2002 Winter Olympics in Salt Lake City, Utah.

NIJ sponsored a groundbreaking study to design a bomb robot built to the specifications of practitioners on the front lines. A technical working group helped define the specifications and identified shortfalls in the current generation of bomb robots. The first commercial device built to meet the working group specifications—called the Vanguard Robot—was introduced in 11 law enforcement agencies in 2002 for testing and operation.

## Securing aircraft

Airline safety became an issue of paramount concern in 2002. Could a stun gun or other less-than-lethal device help a crew member thwart an onboard attack? In FY

*Quick access to numerous manuals, charts, and publications in a wireless palm-sized device gives bomb technicians an edge in performing their dangerous tasks more safely and effectively.*

5

2002, Congress directed NIJ to assess the use of less-than-lethal weapons aboard commercial aircraft as a means of incapacitating individuals posing a clear and present danger. NIJ considered each of the six general categories of less-than-lethal weapons in use or development:

- Electric shock.
- Chemical.
- Impact projectile.
- Physical restraint.
- Light.
- Acoustic.

Many characteristics of an airliner in flight—confined space, air that is recirculated, critical electrical navigation and communication equipment, close proximity of passengers—pose special challenges for each type of weapon.

NIJ's report concluded that electric shock systems, such as tasers or stun guns, show the most promise for use within the confines of an aircraft, but that substantial testing needs to be done to ensure that use of an electrical shock device will not damage or disable critical flight systems. The report cautioned that all of the weapon types pose safety or effectiveness issues that must be thoroughly examined before any deployment is considered.

As Congress considered whether to allow properly trained pilots to have access to firearms as a last line of defense, NIJ, at the request of the Federal Aviation Administration, began developing performance standards for frangible ammunition. Because frangible ammunition by nature more readily breaks into smaller pieces on impact, it would be more suitable for use in an aircraft than other ammunition types.

---

**For more information:**

- NIJ Director Sarah V. Hart's statement to the House Subcommittee on Aviation, Committee on Transportation and Infrastructure, summarizes the report on less-than-lethal weapons (see http://www.ojp.usdoj.gov/nij/speeches/aviation.htm).

- NIJ's Standards and Testing Program is described at http://www.ojp.usdoj.gov/nij/sciencetech/st.htm.

# Violence Against Women/ Family Violence

Since passage of Title IV of the Violent Crime Control and Law Enforcement Act of 1994, NIJ has aggressively sought to identify and fill gaps in knowledge related to violence against women and family violence. Research findings can help bolster the ability of the criminal justice system to protect victims of domestic violence.

## When domestic violence and child maltreatment co-occur (Greenbook initiative)

Too often, domestic violence and child maltreatment occur under the same roof. Yet communities continue to treat violence against women and child maltreatment within the same family as separate problems, addressed by separate systems. As a result, the community response may not be as effective as it could be. To address this, the National Council of Juvenile and Family Court Judges released a report, entitled *Effective Interventions in Domestic Violence and Child Maltreatment: Guidelines for Policy and Practice*, nicknamed the Greenbook.

The Greenbook provides a series of recommendations on how to address domestic violence and child maltreatment simultaneously. The goal is to give courts, child welfare agencies, and domestic violence service organizations more effective methods of responding to battered women and their maltreated children.

An NIJ-backed effort applied Greenbook recommendations at six sites. A national evaluation was begun in 2002 to measure whether the demonstration sites' collaborative efforts result in system change. Four main areas were targeted: identification of co-occurrence of domestic violence and child maltreatment, collaborative planning and implementation, service system change in policies and procedures, and service system integration.

---

**For more information:**

◻ A description of the Greenbook demonstration project is on NIJ's Violence Against Women and Family Violence program Web page, http://www.ojp.usdoj.gov/nij/vawprog/demo_green.html.

## Responding to campus sexual assault

National studies show that college women face a high risk of sexual victimization. Previous NIJ-sponsored research estimated that for every 1,000 women attending a college or university, 35 rapes occur each academic year. (See "For more information" on page 8.)

Groundbreaking NIJ-sponsored research completed in 2002 provided the first comprehensive, national-level investigation of how the Nation's colleges and universities respond to student allegations of rape and sexual assault. The study showed that schools have made progress developing explicit sexual assault prevention and response policies, including making them accessible to students. But only a quarter of all schools routinely use procedures for investigating reports or collecting evidence once a report is made, and only a third use due process procedures for the accused.

The study raised many important questions for college administrators about how sexual assault is handled on their campuses. Although the study's findings revealed some shortcomings in various campus sexual assault policies throughout the Nation, it also provided several practical recommendations to use in developing model sexual assault policies and prevention programs, such as:

◻ Make victims' needs a first priority in the process.

◻ Develop a model sexual assault policy manual.

◻ Develop a model sexual assault education pamphlet for students.

◻ Develop model services for victims.

*Groundbreaking NIJ-sponsored research completed in 2002 provided the first comprehensive, national-level investigation of how the Nation's colleges and universities respond to student allegations of rape and sexual assault.*

This study met the needs of college administrators, campus prevention programmers, and campus law enforcement agencies by providing examples of promising sexual assault programs and emerging policies and practices that are already working to make campuses safer. The final report will be released in 2003.

---

**For more information:**

▫ Bonnie S. Fisher, Francis T. Cullen, and Michael G. Turner, *The Sexual Victimization of College Women*, Washington, DC: U.S. Department of Justice, National Institute of Justice, December 2000 (NCJ 182369), http://www.ojp.usdoj. gov/nij/pubs-sum/182369.htm.

## Transferring child protective investigations to law enforcement

Florida was the first State in the country to pass legislation to allow the entire responsibility for child protective investigations to be transferred from the child welfare system to the criminal justice system. NIJ research measured the outcomes when responsibility for investigations was transferred to the Sheriffs' Office. The research compared counties where the task was handled by child welfare agencies with counties where it was handled by the sheriff. The aim was to see if children are safer and whether there are impacts on other parts of the child welfare system. Findings suggest there is no evidence that the transfer of responsibility for child protection to law enforcement has an effect on children or families, an important finding if such transfers

become a trend because many were concerned that law enforcement would not be as sensitive in handling such cases, resulting in unintended harm. In fact, police officers developed greater sensitivity toward child welfare cases after the transfer of responsibility, focusing on how to help the families involved.

## Research on the commercial sexual exploitation of children

Although the precise number of victims cannot be determined, NIJ research in 2002 estimated that more than 200,000 American children and youth are at risk of commercial sexual exploitation each year. Researchers combined interviews with 1,000 key informants with surveys of nearly 300 agencies that serve child victims and their families to identify the nature and extent of child sexual exploitation. Among the factors fueling child sexual exploitation are prostitution by runaways, prior history of child sexual abuse or assault, poverty, membership in gangs, organized crime recruitment of children for prostitution, and illegal trafficking of children for sexual purposes to the United States from developing countries.

The report offered a series of recommendations to strengthen the Nation's capacity for protecting vulnerable youth from commercial sexual exploitation: emphasize prevention, target the exploiters, enact tougher penalties and wield existing laws more forcefully, and promote public-private partnerships and multijurisdictional task forces to combat exploitation.

# Using Science and Technology to Improve Criminal Justice

NIJ continued its leadership role in developing, testing, and evaluating technology tools to assist criminal justice. Ongoing projects highlight the value of technology in investigating crime, protecting officers and citizens, and detecting illegal and dangerous materials.

## Reducing the DNA testing backlog

Forensic DNA evidence can be a powerful tool to convict the guilty and to exonerate the innocent. But as legislation increases the list of crimes for which offender DNA samples must be collected and law enforcement becomes better trained and equipped to collect DNA samples at crime scenes, the backlog of samples awaiting testing throughout the criminal justice system will continue to increase. NIJ explored ways to reduce the backlog and equip laboratories to manage the influx of convicted offender samples and other casework.

Through the DNA Backlog Reduction Program, NIJ has funded the analysis of almost 500,000 DNA samples taken from convicted offenders in 45 States through fiscal year 2002. Since the program's inception in 2000, the analysis of these samples has generated nearly 2,000 "hits," or matches, with crime scene samples in the State and national DNA databases. Each hit can assist investigators by linking related crimes, proving the innocence of a subject under investigation or even convicted of the crime, or helping to bring a violent criminal to justice.

To take advantage of economies of scale available from the private sector, NIJ has worked with the States to pool samples for analysis by high-capacity private DNA laboratories and by State and local laboratories in order to help make analytic services available at a lower cost. NIJ also screens vendor laboratories to ensure technical capability and quality control, taking this burden off State and local laboratories. As a result, NIJ has reduced the average cost of analysis per sample by more than 30 percent.

During 2002, NIJ restructured the Convicted Offender Backlog Reduction Program to allow States to use private labs selected by the General Services Administration and take advantage of their high capacities. The goal was to make analytic services available more quickly and cost-effectively to State and local laboratories.

**For more information:**

- Visit NIJ's program page on investigative and forensic sciences at http://www.ojp.usdoj.gov/nij/sciencetech/ifs.htm.

## Detecting crack and other smokable forms of cocaine

Federal legislators have set more severe punishments for crack use and trafficking than for powder cocaine use and trafficking. But a lab technician testing an arrestee's urine sample for cocaine use would be unable to tell whether or not the drug was smoked. That may soon change. In 2002, NIJ

9

*NIJ staff, working with a commercial laboratory, announced the discovery that two chemical byproducts of smoked cocaine can be detected through urinalysis. The presence of either of these chemicals has been shown to accurately indicate that cocaine was recently smoked.*

staff, working with a commercial laboratory, announced the discovery that two chemical byproducts of smoked cocaine can be detected through urinalysis. The presence of either of these chemicals has been shown to accurately indicate that cocaine was recently smoked.

Crack is the primary form of smokable cocaine and is considered by many law enforcement officials to be more dangerous than powder cocaine. In addition to being highly addictive, crack is associated with a multitude of social, economic, and health problems.

Although the methodology needs further refining before large-scale testing can be implemented, the ability to distinguish how cocaine is used will enable researchers to verify the accuracy of self-reports in specific populations (e.g., juveniles) and to better analyze drug use trends in the effort to better understand why treatment fails and arrestees recidivate. In addition, improved data could help local officials track the spread of crack in areas where the drug is not well established.

### Technology to search, protect, and communicate

In 2002, NIJ continued to assess and test innovative technologies of practical use to the criminal justice field and to assist in commercializing those technologies that can improve criminal justice.

**Seeing through walls.** Soon law enforcement officers may have the ability to see through solid walls. In 2002, NIJ oversaw the completion of a second-generation prototype of through-the-wall personnel

detection and tracking radar. A number of similar devices are in the development and testing stages. The devices use technology similar to that found in CAT scans or ultrasound equipment to locate and track people through the walls of buildings. If commercialized, such a device could greatly enhance the ability of police to successfully resolve hostage situations.

**Detecting weapons and drugs.** A number of workable technologies are in use to detect weapons at security checkpoints in airports, courts, prisons, and schools. The current generation of devices is limited by a high number of false positives. NIJ continued an assessment of a weapons detection portal in a New York City high school. The portal shows the potential for developing a more reliable system for distinguishing between dangerous weapons and innocuous items such as coins or keys.

Another NIJ-sponsored experiment in 2002 tested drug detection technologies for prison mail rooms. The equipment can help reduce the amount of illicit drugs reaching prisoners in the Nation's prisons and jails.

**Improving communications.** NIJ continued initiatives to improve communications within and among local and regional law enforcement agencies. In 2002, a regional information sharing system for law enforcement was launched in the Hampton Roads, Virginia, area. Another project led to the development of a statewide secure counterterrorism Web site for the Florida Department of Law Enforcement.

**Search and rescue needs.**
NIJ began a project with the U.S. Department of Energy's Savannah River Technology Center in 2002 to identify what technology tools urban search-and-rescue teams can use to perform their job more effectively. The Center collaborated with the Federal Emergency Management Agency and practitioners to determine the needs of the field as a first step in making those

## NATIONAL LAW ENFORCEMENT AND CORRECTIONS TECHNOLOGY CENTER

NIJ's National Law Enforcement and Corrections Technology Center (NLECTC) provides technology assistance along with scientific and engineering advice and support to State and local law enforcement and corrections agencies. NLECTC activities during FY 2002 included:

**Assistance to the Integrated Border Enforcement Teams.** NLECTC helped the Integrated Border Enforcement Teams identify current and emerging technologies for border security applications in such areas as sensors and surveillance, intrusion and human presence detection, geographic information systems (GIS) and related crime mapping technologies, criminal information sharing systems, and less-than-lethal technologies designed to stop boats and other vehicles.

**Assistance to the Metro Area Sniper Task Force.** During the serial sniper incident in the Washington, D.C., metropolitan area, NIJ—through the NLECTC system—offered assistance to the Joint Operations Center, organized by the Montgomery County, Maryland, Police Department to handle the investigation. NLECTC provided hardware, software, and system installation support for the analysis of investigative information; communications interoperability support; and audio/video and timeline analysis.

**Security at the Winter Olympic Games.** To assist with security at the Winter Olympic Games, NLECTC provided the U.S. Forest Service with five thermal imagers to help ensure public safety through wide-area surveillance capability.

**Technology evaluation.** The NLECTC system continued to help State and local agencies avoid costly and potentially harmful mistakes by evaluating manufacturers' technology claims. Of note, the explosive detection capability of the "MOLE" Programmable Detection System was tested, and the device was found to "perform no better than a random selection process."

**Mock Disaster.** NLECTC sponsored the first annual Mock Disaster, which provides comprehensive educational and operational training for emergency first responders to help them plan for, evaluate, respond to, and mitigate large-scale disasters.

**For more information:**

Visit the NLECTC Web page at http://www.justnet.org.

technologies available. Areas of interest include robotics, communications, and technologies to locate individuals in rubble.

**ID checks for inmates.** Biometrics uses physical traits (such as fingerprints, voice analysis, facial features, or eye patterns) to identify an individual. Can biometrics be used effectively in a prison setting? NIJ teamed with the Space and Naval Warfare Systems Center to conduct a biometrics field test at the Naval Correctional Facility in Charleston, South Carolina. The project sought to determine which biometric techniques work best in a prison or jail environment and whether existing technologies need to be modified to meet the special needs of prisons and jails.

Five different biometric technologies have been evaluated, with mixed results. Preliminary results concluded that iris recognition is the most accurate method, while facial recognition produces the most mismatches. But the project underscored that biometrics is an emerging technology with limits. A corrections administrator must weigh that fact and a number of other factors before considering the viability of biometrics in a prison setting. What are the lighting conditions? How many users will there be? Will the device be used overtly or covertly? These and other factors will influence the effectiveness of any technology implemented.

In 2002, NIJ continued a similar project to test biometrics in the Prince Georges County, Maryland, jail.

*During natural disasters, high-speed pursuits, terrorist attacks, or other critical incidents that span jurisdictional boundaries, the ability to communicate can be a matter of life and death.*

**For more information:**

▪ To learn more about biometrics, visit the *Biometrics Catalog* at http://www.biometricscatalog.org, developed with support from NIJ.

**AGILE for interoperability**

During natural disasters, high-speed pursuits, terrorist attacks, or other critical incidents that span jurisdictional boundaries, the ability to communicate can be a matter of life and death. NIJ's AGILE Program was developed to improve the ability of State and local law enforcement agencies to communicate with one another across agency and jurisdictional boundaries. In 2002, the AGILE Program supported the National Task Force on Interoperability, a group formed by 18 national associations representing State and local elected and appointed officials and public safety personnel, with a stated goal of improving interoperability among Federal, State, regional, and local government and public safety agencies. Other AGILE activities in 2002 included:

▪ Funding the development of the Computer-Assisted Precoordination Resource and Database System, which helps agencies in the same geographic region coordinate the allotment of communications airwave frequencies and is used in developing State or regional communication plans.

▪ Providing standards development and support for projects to improve broadband communications, to use wireless technology, and to staff the Nation's communications centers.

- Providing continued support to the National Public Safety Telecommunications Council, the national voice for State and local public safety communications issues.

- Managing a grant to the Capital Wireless Integrated Network, which is creating the first multi-

State, interjurisdictional integrated wireless network in the United States.

---

**For more information:**

- Visit the AGILE Web site at http://www.agileprogram.org.

## Protecting Communities

NIJ continued to explore strategies for keeping communities safe in 2002 by giving communities evidence-based knowledge, innovative methods, and other tools to help reduce crime and protect citizens.

### Reducing firearms violence

Projects in Atlanta, Boston, Detroit, Indianapolis, Los Angeles, and St. Louis have shown some success in targeting and reducing youth gun violence. These six cities operated local projects designed to reduce firearm-related violence and were funded by NIJ, the Office of Community Oriented Policing Services, and the Centers for Disease Control and Prevention.

Lessons learned from these projects are chronicled in a series of publications on reducing gun violence. The first one described Boston's Operation Ceasefire. The second described the Indianapolis Police Department's Directed Patrol Project, which showed that targeted patrol efforts can significantly reduce violent crime. One area of the city, the East District, increased officer contact with citizens, primarily through

increased traffic enforcement. The North District increased officer contact only with targeted individuals who police suspected of being involved in illegal activities. The North District issued far fewer citations, but made twice as many arrests per vehicle stopped and discovered three times as many guns per stop compared to the East District.

Each subsequent report in the series will describe in detail the problem targeted; the program designed to address it; the problems confronted in designing, implementing, and evaluating the effort; and the strategies adopted in responding to any obstacles encountered.

---

**For more information:**

- Edmund F. McGarrell, Steven Chermak, and Alexander Weiss, *Reducing Gun Violence: Evaluation of the Indianapolis Police Department's Directed Patrol Project*, Washington, DC: U.S. Department of Justice, National Institute of Justice, November 2002 (NCJ 188740), http://www.ojp.usdoj.gov/nij/pubs-sum/188740.htm.

*A particular problem in responding to gang-related violence is the lack of valid baseline data on gang incidents. Without accurate information on when and where gang crimes occur, it is difficult to evaluate the effectiveness of anti-gang strategies.*

## Understanding gangs and gang-related crime

Concern about gang-related homicide and violence has reemerged in the last few years. For example, Los Angeles has witnessed a spike in gang-related homicide. Police suspect that more than half of their 658 homicides in 2002 were gang-related. A particular problem in responding to gang-related violence is the lack of valid baseline data on gang incidents. Without accurate information on when and where gang crimes occur, it is difficult to evaluate the effectiveness of anti-gang strategies.

In 2002, NIJ completed research on a regional gang incident tracking system developed in Orange County, California, using geographic information systems (GIS) technology. The system was designed to present a clearer picture of the nature and scope of gang crime and to better track the success of prevention and control efforts.

The research found that the gang incident tracking system presents a relatively unbiased and complete picture of gang incidents handled by the police and that police are not overestimating gang-related crime in Orange County, as some suspected. Instead, the research found that law enforcement agencies tended to underreport gang incidents to the tracking database.

The police logged an average of 3,000 gang-related incidents yearly between 1994 and 2000; about half of these were violent offenses, followed in frequency by vandalism/graffiti, weapons violations, property crimes, and narcotics sales. Trends in the timing and nature of incidents were found, providing a valuable tool to law enforcement and others developing prevention and enforcement strategies.

Other gang studies completed by NIJ covered topics such as gang prevention, female involvement in gangs, youth gang violence problem solving, and links between gangs and organized crime.

**For more information:**

▫ Winifred L. Reed and Scott H. Decker, eds., *Responding to Gangs: Evaluation and Research*, Washington, DC: U.S. Department of Justice, National Institute of Justice, July 2002 (NCJ 190351), http://www.ojp.usdoj.gov/nij/pubs-sum/190351.htm.

## Project Safe Neighborhoods

Project Safe Neighborhoods (PSN) is a comprehensive, multiagency problem-solving Federal initiative designed to reduce firearms violence in each of the 94 U.S. Attorney districts nationwide. Taking the most successful elements of deterrence-based programs in Boston, Richmond, and 10 Strategic Approaches to Community Safety Initiative (SACSI) cities, PSN represents a "new way of doing business" for most criminal justice officials. For this reason, training and technical assistance is critical to the successful implementation of the PSN initiative. As a result, NIJ awarded a grant in 2002 to create a "Project Safe Neighborhoods Academy" to provide this research-based training and assistance.

Goals of the PSN academy include:

- Conducting regional training programs for PSN task forces and their research partners.

- Producing online training modules to support the regional training and manage an online help desk and information clearinghouse.

- Establishing a national cadre of researchers and practitioners with expertise in the problem-solving model to provide technical assistance to the PSN sites as needed.

- Developing a database of common enforcement and intervention activities, measurement instruments, and violence indicator measures.

- Conducting case studies to identify lessons learned and promising approaches.

- Coordinating activities among all the PSN partners and providing frequent feedback to them on all aspects of academy activities and findings.

*By the end of 2002, 70 percent of NIJ's 39,000 registered users had provided an email address in addition to a regular mailing address. More and more of NIJ's audience was equipped and willing to receive information electronically instead of through paper copy.*

## Helping Knowledge Travel Faster, Farther

### Redesigning NIJ's print and electronic products

In 2002, NIJ improved its communications with the public by revising the way it writes and presents its publications. NIJ placed greater emphasis on clear, concise writing with a greater use of plain language and less use of jargon and technical terms. Products more clearly state the relevance of the findings, and distribution is better tailored to specific audiences of State and local practitioners, policymakers, and researchers.

Part of the redesign involved changing the format of the printed documents and the appearance of the Web. Complementary changes were made in the look of CD covers, seminar flyers, conference materials, and other items.

### Reaching out electronically

NIJ took steps in 2002 to become better equipped to reach its audience electronically. Through the National Criminal Justice Reference Service (NCJRS), NIJ maintains a list of registered users—individuals who have asked to receive NIJ materials and have supplied their areas of interest, organizational affiliation, job description, and address. By the end of 2002, 70 percent of NIJ's 39,000 registered users had provided an email address in addition to a regular mailing address. More and more of NIJ's audience was equipped and willing to receive information electronically instead of through paper copy.

### Spreading research results

Findings from NIJ research have always been available through the archives and searchable database at NCJRS. In 2002, NIJ took steps to make all final reports prepared by its grantees available online at the NCJRS Web site. In addition, work began on scanning past grantee final reports so that they too are available electronically.

---

**For more information:**

- Visit the NCJRS Web site, http://www.ncjrs.org.

15

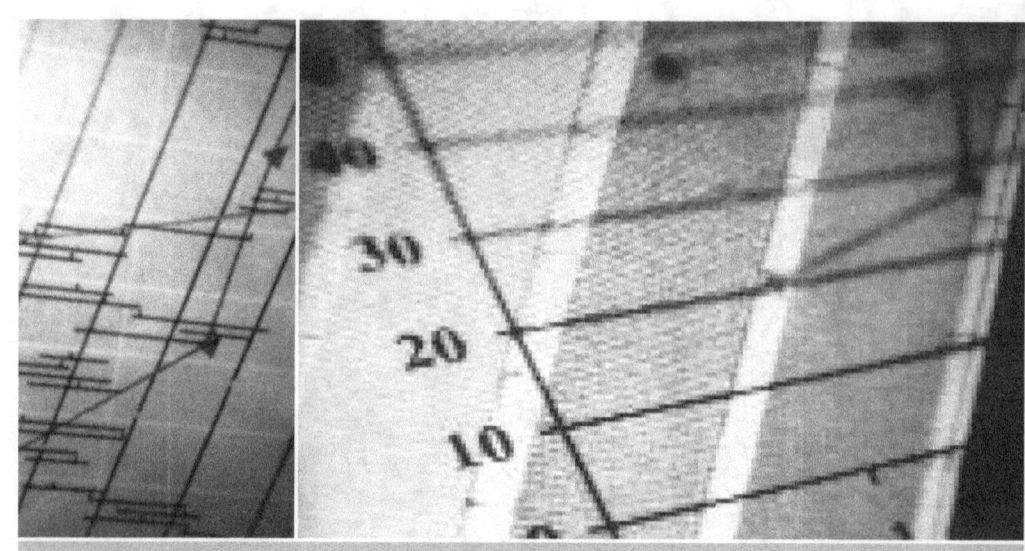

Appendixes

APPENDIX A

# Financial Data

EXHIBIT 1: TRENDS IN NIJ'S RESEARCH AND DEVELOPMENT PORTFOLIO,
FY 1994–2002

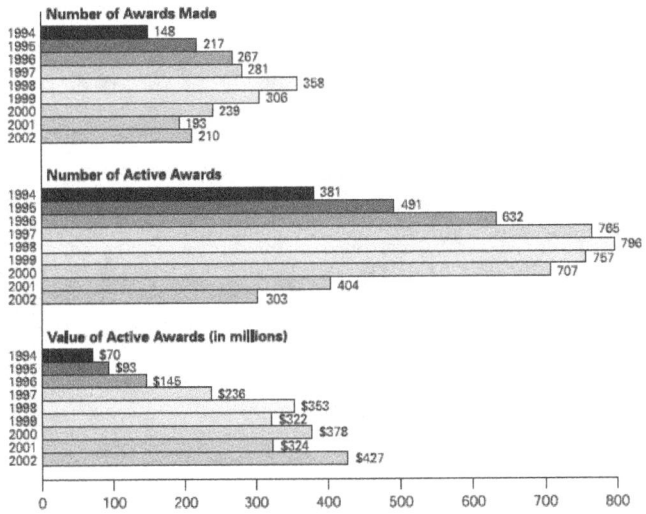

EXHIBIT 2: SOURCES OF NIJ FUNDS, IN MILLIONS, FY 1994–2002

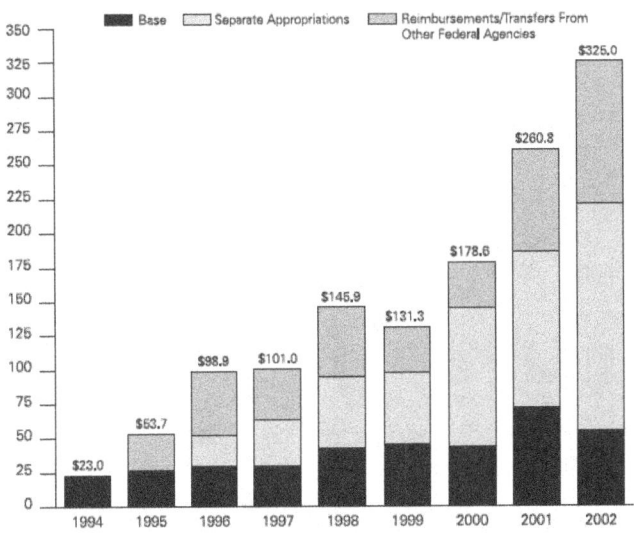

EXHIBIT 3: ALLOCATION OF NIJ FUNDS AS A PERCENTAGE OF
TOTAL EXPENDITURES,* FY 2002

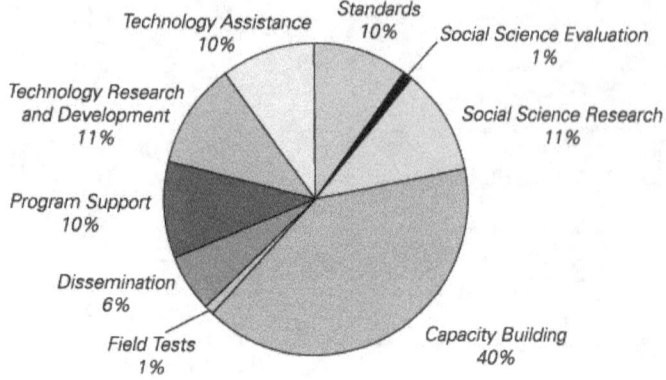

*Total expenditures of $325 million includes NIJ's base appropriation of $54.9 million plus
separate appropriations and funds transferred from other agencies.

APPENDIX B

# NIJ Awards in FY 2002

(includes first-time awards and supplements to previous awards)

## COMMUNITY JUSTICE

**Community Mapping, Planning, and Analysis for Safety Strategy**
Seattle, City of
Gerard Sidorowicz
$400,000                    2000–IJ–CX–K001

**Influences of Community Context on the Processing and Sentencing of Felony Defendants in 54 U.S. Counties**
University of Missouri
Noelle Fearn
$15,000                     2002–IJ–CX–0003

**Measuring the Impact of Collaboration on Community Safety Problem-Solving Initiatives**
Myra Wall Downing
$150,589                    2002–IJ–CX–0024

**Program on Human Development in Chicago Neighborhoods**
Harvard College
Felton Earls
$230,000                    1993–IJ–CX–K005

**Research Partner: East Valley COMPASS (Crime Mapping, Planning, and Analysis for Safety Strategies) Initiative**
Police Foundation
Rachel Boba
$274,560                    2002–MU–CX–K013

**Strengthening and Rebuilding Tribal Justice Systems, Phase II**
University of Arizona
Steven Cornell
$574,519                    2002–MU–MU–0015

## CORRECTIONS

**Breaking the Cycle Demonstration Project**
Jacksonville Department of Community Affairs
Harry Ivey, Jr.
$500,000                    1998–IJ–CX–K013

**Connecticut Correctional Health Research Program**
University of Connecticut Health Center
Robert L. Trestman
$3,000,000                  2002–IJ–CX–K009

**Corrections and Law Enforcement Family Support: Corrections Field Test Design**
Abt Associates Inc.
David Hayeslip
$149,995                    2000–FS–VX–K003

**Evaluation of Drug Treatment at the State Correctional Institution at Chester: A Partnership Between the Pennsylvania Department of Corrections, Gaudenzia, Inc., and Temple University**
Temple University
Wayne Welsh
$376,180                    2002–RT–BX–1002

**Evaluation of the Rhode Island Probation Specialized Domestic Violence Supervision Unit**
Council of State Governments/American Probation and Parole Association
Carl Wicklund
$300,000                    2002–WG–BX–0011

**Examination of Privatization in the Federal Bureau of Prisons**
Abt Associates Inc.
Douglas McDonald
$239,078                    1999–IJ–CX–K018

**Geographic Tools to Improve Officer Safety in Correctional Institutions**
Temple University
George F. Rengert
$397,394                    2002–MU–MU–0016

**Improving Correctional Officer Safety: Reducing Inmate Weapons**
Johns Hopkins University
Donald Dow
$225,516                    2002–IJ–CX–K017

**Neuropsychological and Emotional Deficits Predict Correctional Treatment Response**
Research Triangle Institute
Diana Fishbein
$627,990                    2002–MU–BX–0013

**Providing Transitional Services to Improve Offender Outcomes**
Vera Institute of Justice, Inc.
James Wilson
$375,000                    2002–RT–BX–1001

**Supermax Prisons**
Urban Institute
Dan Mears
$298,127                    2002–IJ–CX–0019

**Working With Technology in Corrections**
American Correctional Association
R.J. Verdeyen
$99,084                     1996–LB–VX–K004

## COURTS

**Evaluation of a Multisite Demonstration for Enhanced Judicial Oversight**
Urban Institute
Adele Harrell
$1,700,000                 1999–WT–VX–K005

**Examining the Collateral Costs of Establishing Specialized Courts**
Justice Management Institute
Douglas K. Somerlot
$300,000                   2002–IJ–CX–K011

**Testing the Effects of Selected Jury Trial Innovations on Juror Comprehension of DNA Evidence**
B. Michael Dann
$213,418                   2002–IJ–CX–0026

**Web-Based Automated System**
Access Justice
Alan Kalmanoff
$175,000                   2002–IJ–CX–K003

## CRIME MAPPING

**Development of an Offender Travel Model for Use in Metropolitan Crime Mapping Systems and Its Integration Into the CrimeStat Spatial Statistics Package**
Ned Levine and Associates
Ned Levine
$111,974                   2002–IJ–CX–0007

**Robust Spatial Analysis Rare Crimes Modeling**
Urban Institute
Avinash Bhati
$58,505                    2002–IJ–CX–0006

## CRIME PREVENTION

**Evaluation of Breaking the Cycle**
Urban Institute
Adele Harrell
$9,999                     1997–IJ–CX–0013

**An Evidence-Based Review of Rape and Sexual Assault Preventive Intervention Program**
Research Triangle Institute
Shannon Morrison
$230,358                   2002–WG–BX–0006

**Rape Prevention Through Bystander Education**
University of New Hampshire
Victoria Banyard
$283,038                   2002–WG–BX–0009

**Screening for Co-Occuring Mental Health and Substance Abuse**
University of Akron
Sonia A. Alemagno
$26,761                    2002–IJ–CX–0028

## CRIMINAL JUSTICE RESEARCH, GENERAL

**Comparative Analysis of Structural Covariates of Female/Male Offending Rates**
Pennsylvania State University
Jennifer Schwarts
$20,000                    2002–IJ–CX–0025

**Enhancing Imputation Methodologies for County-Level UCR Data**
University of Illinois
Michael Maltz
$49,611                    2001–IJ–CX–0006

## DRUGS AND CRIME

**Impact of Alcohol and Drug Use and Criminal Justice Involvement on the Family**
San Francisco State University
Bruce A. Macher
$29,171                    2002–IJ–CX–0030

**A Qualitative Study of Ecstacy Sellers**
Scientific Analysis Corporation
Sheigla Murphy
$583,470                   2002–IJ–CX–0018

## INTERNATIONAL CRIME

**Corruption and the Rule of Law: Dealing With Cultural Differences in the Former Soviet Union**
George Mason University
Janine Wedel
$186,113                   2002–IJ–CX–0017

**NIJ-Rule of Law Transition Support Activities**
Abt Associates Inc.
Terence Dunworth
$299,875                   2001–IJ–CX–K002

## LEGISLATION, POLICY, AND STANDARDS

**Criminology and Public Policy**
American Society of Criminology
Chris Eskridge
$165,917                   2001–IJ–CX–0015

**State Legislative Information and Training**
National Conference of State Legislators
Donna Lyons
$43,312                    2002–IJ–CX–0014

## POLICING

### Policing, General

**Investigation and Prosecution of Homicide Cases in the United States**
Justice Studies, Inc.
Phyllis Newton
$643,349                   2002–IJ–CX–0021

**Policing in the United States: Developing a Comprehensive Model**
Illinois State University
L. Edward Wells
$34,955                    2002–IJ–CX–0016

### Family Support and Stress Management

**Correction Officer Stress Management**
New Jersey Department of Corrections
William Hepner
$97,014                    2001–LT–BX–K013

**Corrections and Law Enforcement Family Support: Law Enforcement Field Test Supplement**
Abt Associates Inc.
David Hayeslip
$150,000                   2000–FS–VX–K004

**Iowa Department of Corrections Staff and Family Support Program**
Iowa Department of Corrections
Larry Brimeyer
$100,000                   2001–LT–BX–K012

**Law Enforcement and Family Stress**
Duluth, City of
Peg Johnson
$100,000                   2001–FS–BX–K002

**North Miami Beach Police "SOS" Stop Our Stress**
North Miami Beach, City of
Venetia Coffey
$80,985                    2001–FS–BX–K003

**Wisconsin Youth Counselor Stress Reduction Program**
Wisconsin Department of Corrections
Shelly Hagan
$100,000                   2001–FS–BX–K001

## SCHOOLS

**Safe Kids, Safe Schools: Evaluating the Use of Iris Recognition Technology**
21st Century Solutions
Craig Uchida
$148,997                   2002–RD–CX–K002

**Safe Schools, Law Enforcement, and Corrections Research Support**
George Mason University
Stephen D. Mastrofski
$149,933                   2000–RD–CX–K003

**School Safety Web-Based Curriculum for Six Target Audiences**
Johns Hopkins University
Jocelyn Bauer
$1,398,799                 2002–RD–CX–K001

**Teacher-Parent Authorization Security System (T-PASS)**
Plumstead Township Board of Education
Philip J. Meara
$293,360                   2002–RD–CX–K005

## SENTENCING

**Investigation and Prosecution of Homicide: Examining the Federal Death Penalty System**
Rand Corporation
Stephen Klein
$1,332,979                 2002–IJ–CX–0022

**Of Fragmentation and Ferment: State Sentencing and Correction**
Vera Institute of Justice
James Wilson
$268,383                   2002–IJ–CX–0027

**Relationship Between Race, Ethnicity, and Sentencing Outcome**
University of Maryland—College Park
Ojmarrh Mitchell
$85,507                    2002–IJ–CX–0020

## TECHNOLOGY DEVELOPMENT

### Officer Protection and Crime Prevention Technologies

**Build a Prototype Optical Recognition System to Identify and Track Stolen Vehicles Using License Plate Reading Techniques**
G2 Tactics
Andrew J. Bucholz
$156,773                   2002–LT–BX–K006

**Center for Criminal Justice Technology**
Mitretek Systems, Inc.
Steven Pomerantz
$1,999,744      2001–LT–BX–K002

**Fighting Crime With Advanced Technologies**
Georgia State University
Robert Friedmann
$3,051,999      2002–RG–CX–K005

**Southwest Border States Anti-Drug Information System**
Criminal Information Sharing Alliance
Glen Gillum
$4,100,000      1997–LB–VX–K009

**Testing of Riot Helmets and Face Shields**
Aspen Systems Corporation
Richard Rosenthal
$3,512,330      1996–MU–MU–K011

**To Develop a Comprehensive Suite of "New Technology"**
Association of Public Safety Communications
Officials International, Inc.
Craig M. Jorgensen
$150,000      1997–LB–VX–K002

Investigative and Forensic Sciences

*Forensics and Crime Labs, General*

**ASCLD/LAB Forensic Laboratory Accreditation Expansion**
American Society of Crime
Laboratory Directors
Frank Fitzpatrick
$140,556      2002–LT–BX–K004

**Ballistics Matching Using 3D Images of Bullets and Cartridge Cases**
Intelligent Automation, Inc.
Benjamin Bachrach
$550,000      1997–LB–VX–0008

**Central Gulf Coast Regional Computer Forensics Lab Project**
University of New Orleans
Danielle Trapagnier
$1,000,000      2002–LP–CX–K004

**City of Bellevue Police Department Forensic Services Unit Crime Lab Improvement Project**
Bellevue, City of
Carl Nicoll
$648,570      2002–RC–CX–K003

**Conference on Medicolegal Death Investigation Systems**
National Academy of Sciences
Linda M. Kilroy
$74,986      2002–LT–BX–K002

**Crime Laboratory Improvement Program—Iowa**
Iowa Department of Public Safety
Jerry L. Brown
$947,910      2002–RC–CX–K002

**Crime Laboratory Improvement Program—Mississippi**
Mississippi Department of Public Safety
Kenneth Winter
$99,780      2002–RC–CX–K004

**Crime Laboratory Improvement Program—Ohio**
Ohio Attorney General Bureau of Criminal
Identification and Investigation
Roger Kahn
$799,573      2002–LP–CX–K007

**Crime Laboratory Improvement Program—Rhode Island**
University of Rhode Island
Franca Cirelli
$449,010      2002–RC–CX–K005

**Crime Laboratory Improvement Program—South Carolina**
South Carolina Law Enforcement Division
Lisa Nine
$2,494,500      2000–RC–CX–0023

**Crime Laboratory Improvement Program—Wisconsin**
Wisconsin Department of Justice
Jerome Geurts
$661,000      2002–RC–CX–K001

**Detection of Date Rape Drugs by Capillary Electrochromatography Using Monolithic Polymer Columns**
Ohio University
Bruce McCord
$183,206      2002–MU–MU–K002

**Development of Statistical Methods for Estimating a Minimum Postmortem Interval: An Evaluation Using Insect Growth Data**
University of Alabama—Birmingham
Jeffrey Wells
$219,450      2002–LT–BX–K001

**Digital Photography**
Iowa Governor's Office of Drug Control Policy
Dennis Wiggins
$33,182      2002–DN–BX–0019

**Expanding the Use and Deployment of Imaging Systems in Law Enforcement**
Institute for Forensic Imaging Foundation, Inc.
Herbert Blitzer
$200,000      2002–RG–CX–K004

**Forensic Laboratory Improvement for the State of Alabama**
Alabama Department of Economic and Community Affairs
James H. Fry
$50,676                    2002–DN–BX–1001

**Gene Polymorphism and Human Pigmentation**
University of Arizona
Murray Brilliant
$496,053                   2002–IJ–CX–K010

**Improving Crime Lab Evidence Analysis and Efficiency in Utah**
Utah Commission on Criminal and Juvenile Justice
Richard Ziebarth
$29,178                    2002–DN–BX–0049

**Improving Forensic Science Capabilities in the State of Vermont**
Vermont Department of Public Safety
Eric Buel
$29,178                    2002–DN–BX–0050

**Marshall University Forensic Science Center**
Marshall University Research Corporation
Ron Schelling
$3,493,218                 2001–RC–CX–K002

**Mid-Infrared Cavity Ring-Down Spectroscopy System for Law Enforcement Applications**
BlueLeaf Networks
Thomas G. Owano
$299,932                   2002–MU–CX–K008

**National Center for Forensic Science**
University of Central Florida
Carrie Whitcomb
$1,274,883                 1998–IJ–CX–K003

**National Forensic Science Institute**
University of Tennessee—Knoxville
Michael L. Sullivan
$1,000,000                 2002–LP–CX–K006

**National Forensic Sciences Improvement Act (NFSIA): Increasing Productivity in the Crime Lab Division**
North Dakota, State of
Hope Olson
$29,178                    2002–DN–BX–0038

**Nontoxic Drug Detection and Identification Technology Research Program**
Mistral Security, Inc.
Eyal Banai
$449,991                   2000–RD–CX–K004

**Paul Coverdell National Forensic Sciences Improvement Act (NFSIA) Grant—FY2002**
New York State Division of Criminal Justice Services
John W. Hicks
$215,802                   2002–DN–BX–0036

**Paul Coverdell National Forensic Sciences Improvement Act (NFSIA): Quality System Support Project**
Colorado Division of Criminal Justice
Randy R. Kennedy
$50,146                    2002–DN–BX–0008

**Proficiency Testing and Procedure Validation for Forensic Document Examiners**
Drexel University
Moshe Kam
$296,226                   2002–LT–BX–K008

**Quantitative Assessment of Handwriting**
State University of New York—Albany
Sargur Srihari
$298,237                   2002–LT–BX–K007

**Questioned Document Examination by Laser Desorption Mass Spectrometry**
Michigan State University
John Allison
$212,733                   2002–RB–CX–K002

**Service Quality in Crime Laboratories**
National Forensic Science Technology Center
William J. Tilstone
$8,846,086                 2000–RC–CX–K001

**2002 Forensic Crime Laboratory Improvement Program**
South Carolina Law Enforcement Division
Lisa Nine
$1,750,000                 2002–LP–CX–K002

*Biometrics and Smart Gun Technology*

**Application of Frequency-Based Coding to Smart Gun Technology**
Technology Next, Inc.
Irene Vershinin
$175,856                   2002–IJ–CX–K006

**Creation of a Smart Gun With Radio Frequency Identification**
VLe Small Arms
Arthur D. Schatz
$185,000                   2002–IJ–CX–K021

23

**Development of a Human Skin Biometric Identification System for Authorized User Only Handguns**
Smith & Wesson
Kevin G. Foley
$590,884                2002–IJ–CX–K004

**Face Recognition and Intelligent Software Development**
Analytic Services, Inc.
Timothy Floyd
$1,797,767              1998–LB–VX–K021

**Optical Methods for Authorized Handgun User Recognition**
Exponent, Inc.
Phillip Whitley
$187,598                2002–IJ–CX–K012

**Personalized Firearm Research and Review of Biometric Technology**
iGun Technology Corporation
Jonathan Mossberg
$299,389                2002–IJ–CX–K002

**Squad Car Unit Identification Program**
Ontario, City of
Steven R. Duke
$1,800,000              2002–RG–CX–K006

**Virginia Electronic Fingerprint Archive System**
Virginia Department of State Police
Gunnar G. Kohlbeck
$250,000                2002–LP–CX–K005

*DNA*

**Assessment and *In Vitro* Repair of Damaged DNA Templates**
University of Central Florida
Mary B. Stanley
$115,123                2002–IJ–CX–K001

**A Chip-Based Genetic Detector of Rapid Identification of Individuals**
Nanogen, Inc.
David Yenter
$1,700,000              1997–LB–VX–0004

**DNA Backlog Reduction**
Arkansas State Crime Laboratory
Kenneth H. Michau
$60,000                 2002–LP–CX–K001

**International Association of Chiefs of Police DNA Summit**
International Association of Chiefs of Police
John Firman
$30,000                 2002–VF–GX–K014

**No Suspect Casework DNA Backlog Reduction Program, FY 2001**
Alabama Department of Forensic Sciences
J.C. Upshaw Downs
$690,246                2002–DN–BX–K024

**No Suspect Casework DNA Backlog Reduction Program, FY 2001**
Albuquerque, City of
John Krebsbach
$550,245                2002–DN–BX–K008

**No Suspect Casework DNA Backlog Reduction Program, FY 2001**
Arizona Department of Public Safety
Todd Griffith
$1,052,282              2002–DN–BX–K016

**No Suspect Casework DNA Backlog Reduction Program, FY 2001**
Connecticut Department of Public Safety
Elaine M. Pagliaro
$117,163                2002–DN–BX–K004

**No Suspect Casework DNA Backlog Reduction Program, FY 2001**
Delaware Health and Social Services
Daniel E. Katz
$129,413                2002–DN–BX–K025

**No Suspect Casework DNA Backlog Reduction Program, FY 2001**
Florida Department of Law Enforcement
Suzanne Livingston
$2,795,086              2002–DN–BX–K006

**No Suspect Casework DNA Backlog Reduction Program, FY 2001**
Illinois State Police
Sandra Nelson-Brown
$500,000                2002–DN–BX–K005

**No Suspect Casework DNA Backlog Reduction Program, FY 2001**
Indiana State Police
Paul Misner
$303,558                2002–DN–BX–K015

**No Suspect Casework DNA Backlog Reduction Program, FY 2001**
Institute of Forensic Sciences
Carmen Tirado
$131,678                2002–DN–BX–K020

**No Suspect Casework DNA Backlog Reduction Program, FY 2001**
Kansas Bureau of Investigation
Kyle G. Smith
$377,176                2002–DN–BX–K019

**No Suspect Casework DNA Backlog Reduction Program, FY 2001**
Kentucky State Police
Leslie Gannon
$291,543                2002–DN–BX–K013

No Suspect Casework DNA Backlog
**Reduction Program, FY 2001**
Maine State Police
Timothy D. Kupferschmid
$376,554                2002–DN–BX–K003

No Suspect Casework DNA Backlog
**Reduction Program, FY 2001**
Maryland State Police
Ken Hasenei
$5,048,669              2002–DN–BX–K014

No Suspect Casework DNA Backlog
**Reduction Program, FY 2001**
Massachusetts State Police
Carl M. Selavka
$917,030                2002–DN–BX–K022

No Suspect Casework DNA Backlog
**Reduction Program, FY 2001**
Michigan State Police—Forensic
Science Division
Charles Barna
$1,471,170              2002–DN–BX–K011

No Suspect Casework DNA Backlog
**Reduction Program, FY 2001**
Missouri State Highway Patrol
T.J. Luikart
$348,412                2002–DN–BX–K017

No Suspect Casework DNA Backlog
**Reduction Program, FY 2001**
Nebraska State Patrol
Gale Griess
$226,494                2002–DN–BX–K018

No Suspect Casework DNA Backlog
**Reduction Program, FY 2001**
New Hampshire Department of Safety
Melisa Staples
$71,716                 2002–DN–BX–K001

No Suspect Casework DNA Backlog
**Reduction Program, FY 2001**
New Jersey Department of
Law and Public Safety
Linda Jankowski
$286,805                2002–DN–BX–K007

No Suspect Casework DNA Backlog
**Reduction Program, FY 2001**
New York State Division of
Criminal Justice Services
John W. Hicks
$5,039,535              2002–DN–BX–K021

No Suspect Casework DNA Backlog
**Reduction Program, FY 2001**
Ohio Attorney General Bureau of Criminal
Identification and Investigation
Roger Kahn
$2,254,088              2002–DN–BX–K009

No Suspect Casework DNA Backlog
**Reduction Program, FY 2001**
Oklahoma State Bureau of Investigation
Charles Curtis
$500,000                2002–DN–BX–K010

No Suspect Casework DNA Backlog
**Reduction Program, FY 2001**
Texas Department of Public Safety
J. Ronald Urbanovsky
$3,379,688              2002–DN–BX–K012

No Suspect Casework DNA Backlog
**Reduction Program, FY 2001**
Vermont Department of Public Safety
Eric Buel
$20,829                 2002–DN–BX–K002

No Suspect Casework DNA Backlog
**Reduction Program, FY 2001**
Wisconsin Department of Justice
Jerry Geurts
$1,633,000              2002–DN–BX–K023

**Novel STR Multiplexes With Reduced
Size to Analyze DNA**
Ohio University
Bruce McCord
$453,110                2002–IJ–CX–K007

**Program Acceleration/Enhancements for
Microdevice DNA Forensics System**
Whitehead Institute for Biomedical
Research
Daniel J. Ehrlich
$499,342                1998–LB–VX–K022

**Quantitation of DNA for Forensic
DNA Typing by qPCR**
California Department of Justice
Eva Steinberger
$126,821                2002–IJ–CX–K008

**Research and Development of
Comprehensive Statistical Data**
Smith Alling Lane, PS
Timothy Schellberg
$207,317                2002–LT–BX–K003

**Simple, Rapid, and Accurate
Quantitation of Human DNA**
Vermont Department of Public Safety
Eric Buel
$124,970                2000–IJ–CX–K012

**SNP Detection in Highly Degraded DNA**
University of California—Berkeley
George Sensabaugh
$215,322                2002–IJ–CX–K005

25

Less-Than-Lethal Incapacitation

**Feasibility Study of a Finite Element Model to Assess Less-Than-Lethal Munitions**
Wayne State University
Cynthia Bir
$130,889                2002–LT–BX–K005

**Multisensor Grenade and Field Evaluation**
Scientific Applications and Research Associates, Inc.
Lexi Donne
$125,821                2002–IJ–CX–K014

**Multishot Launcher With Advanced Less-Than-Lethal Ring Airfoil Projectiles**
Vanek Prototype Co.
Chester F. Vanek
$339,000                2002–IJ–CX–K015

**Nonlethal Technologies, Inc., Road Sentry™ Improvement**
Nonlethal Technologies, Inc.
Bradley X. Boyer
$100,000                2002–LT–BX–K009

**Penetration Assessment of Less-Than-Lethal Munitions**
Wayne State University
Cynthia Bir
$202,274                2002–IJ–CX–K020

**Performance Characterization Study of Noise-Flash Diversionary Device**
E-LABS, Inc.
Ronald B. Rise
$151,000                2002–DT–CX–K001

**Variable-Range Less-Lethal Ballistic, Phase II**
Law Enforcement Technologies, Inc.
Greg B. MacAleese
$285,421                2002–MU–MU–K007

Communication and Information Technologies

**Accelerated Information Sharing for Law Enforcement**
National Law Enforcement Telecommunication System
Steven E. Correll
$650,000                2002–MU–MU–K005

**Advanced Generation Interoperability for Law Enforcement Technology**
University of Denver Colorado Seminary
Robert Epper
$1,588,460                2001–RD–CX–K001

**Capital Wireless Integrated Network (CapWIN)**
University of Maryland—College Park
George Ake
$19,246,249                2001–RB–CX–K001

**Capital Wireless Integrated Network (CapWIN) External Policy Development Research**
George Mason University
Roger Stough
$472,500                2002–TE–CX–K002

**Completion of Statewide Interagency Communications System**
South Dakota Highway Patrol
Thomas Dravland
$6,499,669                2002–RG–CX–K002

**Distributed COPLINK Database and Concept Space Development**
Tucson, City of
Jennifer Schroeder
$250,000                2000–RB–CX–K001

**Handheld Front-End for an Enhanced Speech-to-Forms Translation System**
Language Systems, Inc.
Christine Montgomery
$301,846                1999–LT–VX–K025

**Handheld Software Radio for Interoperability**
Andrew D. Beard
$144,252                2002–RD–CX–K004

**Indiana Hoosier Safe-T Project**
Indiana State Police
Lester Miller
$3,000,000                2001–LT–BX–K003

**International Association of Chiefs of Police Technology Information Exchange: Phase III**
International Association of Chiefs of Police
John Firman
$275,000                1999–LT–VX–K004

**JCIT/InfraLynx Operational Assessment**
Johns Hopkins University—Applied Physics Laboratory
Vanu, Inc.
Nicole Nicholson
$90,877                2002–RD–CX–K003

**Law Enforcement Data Mining Analytical Tools**
University of Maryland—College Park
Thomas H. Carr
$1,470,000                1999–LT–VX–K010

**Prehospital, Emergency Medical Services, and Emergency Department Information Interoperability Project for Arlington County**
Silva Consulting Services, LLC
John S. Silva
$148,132                      2002–RD–CX–K006

**Public Safety Partnership/Project Mesa**
Telecommunication Industry Association
Dan Bart
$150,000                      2002–RG–CX–K008

**State Leadership in Public Safety Wireless Interoperability**
National Governors' Association Center for Best Practices
Thom Robel
$150,000                      2002–RG–CX–K001

**Statewide LAWNET Communications Project**
New Hampshire Department of Safety
Frederick H. Booth
$4,000,000                    2001–MU–MU–K010

**2002 Radio/Communication System Upgrade**
South Carolina Law Enforcement Division
Lisa Nine
$3,000,000                    2002–RG–CX–0005

Training and Simulation Technologies

**Development of Distance Learning Capability**
National Corrections and Law Enforcement Training and Technology Center
G. Steve Morrison
$900,000                      2001–LT–BX–K007

**Law Enforcement Technology Dissemination and Training**
Eastern Kentucky University
James Thurman
$221,164                      2000–MU–MU–K008

Program Assessment, Policy, and Coordination

**Project of the Surplus Property Program**
Ultimate Enterprises Limited
Michael Simpson
$246,000                      1996–LB–VX–K002

**Technology and Policy Assessment Executive Panel**
SEASKATE, Inc.
E.A. Burkhalter, Jr.
$533,978                      2001–MU–MU–K003

**Technology and Policy Assessment Liability Task Group**
SEASKATE, Inc.
E.A. Burkhalter, Jr.
$139,681                      2001–MU–MU–K001

Technology Assistance

**Cooperative Truck Stopping**
Aerospace Corporation
Robert Waldron
$2,006,996                    2000–MU–MU–K004

**Operation of the Office of Law Enforcement Technology Commercialization**
Wheeling Jesuit University
Carole Coleman
$2,793,795                    1998–IJ–CX–K002

**Operations of the National Law Enforcement and Corrections Technology Center—Rocky Mountain Region**
University of Denver Colorado Seminary
James Keller
$2,061,832                    1996–MU–MU–K012

**Project Safe Neighborhoods Academy: Proposal to Provide Technical Assistance**
Michigan State University
Edmund McGarrell
$898,233                      2002–GP–CX–1003

**Rural Law Enforcement Technology Center**
Eastern Kentucky University
Pam Collins
$1,529,000                    2001–MU–MU–K009

**Support Services for the National Interoperability Task Force**
Center for Technology Commercialization, Inc.
James Scutt
$275,528                      2001–LT–BX–K011

**Technology Conference/Force Protection Equipment Demonstration Project Support**
Center for Technology Commercialization, Inc.
James Scutt
$507,843                      1999–LT–VX–K021

**Transportation/Information Technology Research Program to Support Capital Wireless Integrated Network (CapWIN)**
University of Virginia
B.L. Smith
$472,500                      2002–TE–CX–K001

## TERRORISM AND CRITICAL INCIDENTS

**Counterterrorism and Cybersecurity Research and Development**
Dartmouth College
Michael Vatis
$35,960,400          2000–DT–CX–K001

**Critical Incident Response Toolset Project**
South Carolina Research Authority
Linda Thomas
$7,591,187          2002–MU–MU–K011

**Impact of Economic, Political, and Social Variables on Incidents of World Terrorism**
University of Maryland—College Park
Gary LaFree
$172,331          2002–DT–CX–0001

**Informal Value Transfer Systems, Terrorism, and Money Laundering**
Temple University
Nickolaos Passas
$119,443          2002–IJ–CX–0001

**Learning From 9/11: Comparative Case Studies of the Law Enforcement Response in New York**
Police Executive Research Forum
Gerald Murphy
$281,466          2002–IJ–CX–0013

**New York University Center for Catastrophe Preparedness Response**
New York University
Robert Berne
$7,000,000          2002–DT–CX–K002

**Oklahoma City National Memorial Institute for the Prevention of Terrorism**
Dennis Reimer
$17,355,400          2000–DT–CX–K0002

**Roundtable on Social and Behavioral Sciences and Terrorism**
National Academy of Sciences
Carol Petrie
$200,000          2002–IJ–CX–0015

## UNEMPLOYMENT AND CRIME

**Consequences of a Criminal Record for Employment Opportunity**
University of Wisconsin—Madison
Devah Pager
$15,000          2002–IJ–CX–0002

**Spatial and Temporal Linkages Between Unemployment and Crime**
Westat, Inc.
Sanjeev Sridharan
$53,610          2002–IJ–CX–0010

## VICTIMIZATION AND VICTIM SERVICES

**Assessment of the State Victim Assistance Academy**
Caliber Associates
Janet Griffith
$390,000          2002–VF–GX–0001

**Criminal Justice Effects of Resource Rape Services**
Sexual Assault and Trauma Center of Rhode Island
Pam Langhammer
$159,614          2002–WG–BX–0007

**Evaluation of Services for Trafficking Victims Discretionary Grant Program**
Caliber Associates
Heather Clawson
$485,663          2002–MU–MU–K004

**Reducing Repeat Sexual Assault Victimization: Design and Testing of a Risk Reduction Program in an Urban Sample**
Vera Institute of Justice, Inc.
Robert C. Davis
$299,990          2002–WG–BX–0008

## VIOLENCE

### Violence Against Women and Family Violence

**Co-Occuring Intimate Partner Violence and Child Maltreatment**
Children's Research Institute
Kelly J. Kelleher
$399,774          2002–WG–BX–0014

**Domestic Violence Against Older Women**
Florida International University
Burton D. Dunlop
$337,973          2002–WG–BX–0010

**Employment, Family, and Social Consequences of Intimate Partner Violence: A Longitudinal Analysis of Impact Over Time**
University of Maryland—College Park
Laura Dugan
$31,234          2002–IJ–CX–0012

**Evaluation of a Multisite Demonstration of Collaborations to Address Domestic Violence and Child Maltreatment**
Caliber Associates
Sharon Bishop
$749,448                    2000–MU–MU–0014

**Experience of Violence in the Lives of Homeless Women**
University of Central Florida
James Wright
$326,033                    2002–WG–BX–0013

**Intimate Partner Violence During Visitation: A Longitudinal Study of Supervised and Unsupervised Access**
Safe Horizon, Inc.
Chris O'Sullivan
$198,946                    2002–WG–BX–0012

**Patterns of Violence Against Women: Risk Factors and Consequences**
University of Minnesota
Ian Macmillan
$33,594                    2002–IJ–CX–0011

**Police Intervention and the Repeat of Domestic Assault**
Pennsylvania State University
Richard Felson
$34,867                    2002–WG–BX–0002

**Sexual Assault Among Intimates: Frequency, Consequences, and Treatments**
Texas Woman's University
Judith McFarlane
$254,322                    2002–WG–BX–0003

**Sexual Assault During and After Separation/Divorce: An Exploratory Study**
Ohio University
Walter DeKeseredy
$104,832                    2002–WG–BX–0004

### Firearms

**Biomechanical Assessment of Blunt Ballistic Impacts to the Abdomen**
Wayne State University
Cynthia Bir
$318,253                    2002–MU–CX–K006

**Firearm Markets and Firearm Violence**
University of California—Davis
Garen Wintemute
$250,000                    2002–IJ–CX–0005

### YOUTH

**Adolescent Victimization and Offending: Specifying the Role of Peer Groups**
Pennsylvania State University
Jennifer Shaffer
$20,000                    2002–IJ–CX–0008

**Breaking the Cycle Project for Juveniles**
Lane County Department of Youth Services
Stephen Carmichael
$1,000,000                    1999–IJ–CX–K017

**Correlates and Consequences of Juvenile Exposure to Violence**
Kansas State University
Stacey Nofziger
$34,980                    2002–IJ–CX–0004

**Risk Management of Sexually-Reactive Children and Adolescents**
Justice Resource Institute, Inc.
Robert Prentky
$284,780                    2002–IJ–CX–0029

APPENDIX C

# NIJ Publications and Products in FY 2002

Most NIJ materials are free and can be obtained from these three sources:

1. NIJ Web page: http://www.ojp.usdoj.gov/nij.

2. National Criminal Justice Reference Service (NCJRS): http://www.ncjrs.org, 800–851–3420, P.O. Box 6000, Rockville, MD 20849–6000.

3. (For science and technology materials) National Law Enforcement and Corrections Technology Center (NLECTC): http://www.justnet.org, 800–248–2742.

## CORRECTIONS

*The I–ADAM in Eight Countries: Approaches and Challenges,* Taylor, Bruce, Progress Report, May 2002, 170 pages, NCJ 189768.

*Implementing Telemedicine in Correctional Facilities,* Nacci, Peter L., C. Allan Turner, Ronald J. Waldron, and Eddie Broyles, Research Report, May 2002, 57 pages, NCJ 190310.

## COURTS

*Documenting Domestic Violence: How Health Care Providers Can Help Victims,* Isaac, Nancy E., and V. Pualani Enos, Research in Brief, September 2001, 10 pages, NCJ 188564.

*The Second Annual National Conference on Science and the Law: Summary of Proceedings,* Research Forum, June 2002, 56 pages, NCJ 191717.

## CRIME PREVENTION

*Community Policing and the "New Immigrants": Latinos in Chicago,* Skogan, Wesley G., Lynn Steiner, Jill DuBois, J. Erik Gudell, and Aimee Fagan, Research Report, July 2002, 19 pages, NCJ 189908.

*Reducing Gun Violence: The Boston Gun Project's Operation Ceasefire,* Kennedy, David M., Anthony A. Braga, Anne M. Piehl, and Elin J. Waring, Research Report, September 2001, 60 pages, NCJ 188741.

*Taking Stock: Community Policing in Chicago,* Skogan, Wesley G., Lynn Steiner, Jill DuBois, J. Erik Gudell, and Aimee Fagan, Research Report, July 2002, 28 pages, NCJ 189909.

## DRUGS AND CRIME

*The I–ADAM in Eight Countries: Approaches and Challenges,* Taylor, Bruce, Progress Report, May 2002, 170 pages, NCJ 189768.

*Toward a Drugs and Crime Research Agenda for the 21st Century,* Research Forum, June 2002, NCJ 194616.

## INVESTIGATIVE SCIENCES

*Second Annual National Conference on Science and the Law: Summary of Proceedings,* Research Forum, May 2002, 56 pages, NCJ 191717.

*Test Results for Disk Imaging Tools: dd GNU fileutils 4.0.36, Provided With Red Hat Linux 7.1,* Special Report, August 2002, 57 pages, NCJ 196352.

## LAW ENFORCEMENT

*Community Policing and the "New Immigrants": Latinos in Chicago,* Skogan, Wesley G., Lynn Steiner, Jill DuBois, J. Erik Gudell, and Aimee Fagan, Research Report, July 2002, 19 pages, NCJ 189908.

*Fighting Crime With COPS and Citizens,* June 2002, http://www.ojp.usdoj.gov/nij/ pubs-sum/cops.htm.

*Guide for the Selection of Chemical Agent and Toxic Industrial Material Detection Equipment for Emergency First Responders,* Volumes 1 and 2, NIJ Guide 100–00, November 2001, 74 pages (Volume 1), 494 pages (Volume 2), NCJ 184449 and 184450.

*Guide for the Selection of Communication Equipment for Emergency First Responders,* Volumes 1 and 2, NIJ Guide 104–00, February 2002, 64 pages (Volume 1), 422 pages (Volume 2), NCJ 191160 and 191161.

*Introduction to Biological Agent Detection Equipment for Emergency First Responders, NIJ Guide 101–00,* NIJ Guide, December 2001, 53 pages, NCJ 190747.

*Pepper Spray's Effects on a Suspect's Ability to Breathe,* Chan, Theodore C., Gary M. Vilke, Jack Clausen, Richard Clark, Paul Schmidt, Thomas Snowden, and Tom Neuman, Research in Brief, December 2001, 8 pages, NCJ 188069.

*Reducing Gun Violence: The Boston Gun Project's Operation Ceasefire,* Kennedy, David M., Anthony A. Braga, Anne M. Piehl, and Elin J. Waring, Research Report, September 2001, 60 pages, NCJ 188741.

*Satisfaction With Police—What Matters?* Reisig, Michael D., Research Report, October 2002, 11 pages, NCJ 194077.

*Selection and Application Guide to Personal Body Armor,* NIJ Guide, November 2001, 121 pages, NCJ 189633.

*Taking Stock: Community Policing in Chicago,* Skogan, Wesley G., Lynn Steiner, Jill DuBois, J. Erik Gudell, and Aimee Fagan, Research Report, July 2002, 28 pages, NCJ 189909.

## RESEARCH AND EVALUATION

*Community Policing and the "New Immigrants": Latinos in Chicago,* Skogan, Wesley G., Lynn Steiner, Jill DuBois, J. Erik Gudell, and Aimee Fagan, Research Report, July 2002, 19 pages, NCJ 189908.

*The I–ADAM in Eight Countries: Approaches and Challenges,* Taylor, Bruce, Progress Report, May 2002, 170 pages, NCJ 189768.

*Implementing Telemedicine in Correctional Facilities,* Nacci, Peter L., C. Allan Turner, Ronald J. Waldron, and Eddie Broyles, Research Report, May 2002, 57 pages, NCJ 190310.

*Pepper Spray's Effects on a Suspect's Ability to Breathe,* Chan, Theodore C., Gary M. Vilke, Jack Clausen, Richard Clark, Paul Schmidt, Thomas Snowden, and Tom Neuman, Research in Brief, December 2001, 8 pages, NCJ 188069.

*Perspectives on Crime and Justice: 2000–2001 Lecture Series, Volume V,* Research Forum, March 2002, 86 pages, NCJ 187100.

*Reducing Gun Violence: The Boston Gun Project's Operation Ceasefire,* Kennedy, David M., Anthony A. Braga, Anne M. Piehl, and Elin J. Waring, Research Report, September 2001, 60 pages, NCJ 188741.

*Satisfaction With Police—What Matters?* Reisig, Michael D., Research Report, October 2002, 11 pages, NCJ 194077.

*Taking Stock: Community Policing in Chicago,* Skogan, Wesley G., Lynn Steiner, Jill DuBois, J. Erik Gudell, and Aimee Fagan, Research Report, July 2002, 28 pages, NCJ 189909.

*Toward a Drugs and Crime Research Agenda for the 21ˢᵗ Century,* Research Forum, June 2002, NCJ 194616.

## SCIENCE AND TECHNOLOGY

*Guide for the Selection of Chemical and Biological Decontamination Equipment for Emergency First Responders, Volumes 1 and 2, NIJ Guide 103–00,* October 2001, 96 pages (Volume 1), 186 pages (Volume 2), NCJ 189724 and 189725.

*Guide for the Selection of Communication Equipment for Emergency First Responders, Volumes 1 and 2, NIJ Guide 104–00,* February 2002, 64 pages (Volume 1), 422 pages (Volume 2), NCJ 191160 and 191161.

*Implementing Telemedicine in Correctional Facilities,* Nacci, Peter L., C. Allan Turner, Ronald J. Waldron, and Eddie Broyles, Research Report, May 2002, 57 pages, NCJ 190310.

*Improved Analysis of DNA Short Tandem Repeats With Time-of-Flight Mass Spectrometry,* Butler, John M., and Christopher H. Becker, Science and Technology Research Report, October 2001, 54 pages, NCJ 188292.

*Introduction to Biological Agent Detection Equipment for Emergency First Responders, NIJ Guide 101–00,* NIJ Guide, December 2001, 53 pages, NCJ 190747.

*Pepper Spray's Effects on a Suspect's Ability to Breathe,* Chan, Theodore C., Gary M. Vilke, Jack Clausen, Richard Clark, Paul Schmidt, Thomas Snowden, and Tom Neuman, Research in Brief, December 2001, 8 pages, NCJ 188069.

*Second Annual National Conference on Science and the Law: Summary of Proceedings,* Research Forum, May 2002, 56 pages, NCJ 191717.

*Selection and Application Guide to Personal Body Armor,* NIJ Guide, November 2001, 121 pages, NCJ 189633.

## NIJ JOURNAL

March 2002, Articles "Prosecutors, Kids, and Domestic Violence Cases" by Debra Whitcomb; "Preventing School Shootings: A Summary of a U.S. Secret Service Safe School Initiative Report"; "Tired Cops: The Prevalence and Potential Consequences of Police Fatigue" by Bryan Vila and Dennis Jay Kenney; "Trust and Confidence in Criminal Justice" by Lawrence W. Sherman, 44 pages, JR 000248.

## SOLICITATIONS FOR RESEARCH AND EVALUATION

*Crime Mapping Research: Funding for Spatial Data Analysis,* June 2001, 8 pages.

*Data Resources Program 2002 Solicitation Funding for the Analysis of Existing Data,* December 2001, 14 pages.

*An Evaluation of Services for Trafficking Victims Discretionary Grant Program: Comprehensive Services Sites,* July 2002, 13 pages.

*Graduate Research Fellowship 2002 Program,* December 2001, 11 pages.

*NIJ Less-Than-Lethal Technology Solicitation, FY 2002,* February 2002, 11 pages.

*NIJ School Safety Technology Solicitation, FY 2002,* February 2002, 14 pages.

*No Suspect Casework DNA Backlog Reduction Program, FY 2001,* May 2002, 34 pages.

*No Suspect Casework DNA Backlog Reduction Program, FY 2003,* May 2002, 34 pages.

*Office of Research and Evaluation 2002 Solicitation for Investigator-Initiated Research,* October 2001, 15 pages.

*Paul Coverdell National Forensic Sciences Improvement Act Grants,* August 2002.

*Science and Technology Solicitation, FY 2002,* February 2002, 13 pages.

*Solicitation for a Research Partner for the East Valley, California, COMPASS (Community Mapping, Planning, and Analysis for Safety Strategies) Initiative,* September 2001.

*Solicitation for Forensic DNA Research and Development, FY 2002,* December 2001, 10 pages.

*Solicitation for Research and Evaluation in Corrections, 2001,* August 2001, 15 pages.

*Solicitation for Research Into the Investigation and Prosecution of Homicide: Examining the Federal Death Penalty System,* July 2001, 16 pages.

*Solicitation for Research on Sexual Violence, FY 2002,* July 2001, 15 pages.

*Solicitation for the Crime Laboratory Improvement Program for FY 2002,* May 2002, 10 pages.

*Violence Against Women Investigator-Initiated Research and Evaluation,* November 2001, 17 pages.

*W.E.B. DuBois Fellowship Program: NIJ Research Opportunity,* December 2001, 15 pages.

TOP 20 NIJ PUBLICATIONS BY NUMBER OF PAPER COPIES DISTRIBUTED, FY 2002

| | Title | Quantity | Year of Publication |
|---|---|---|---|
| 1 | Electronic Crime Scene Investigation: A Guide for First Responders | 24,740 | 2001 |
| 2 | What Every Law Enforcement Officer Should Know About DNA Evidence | 19,822 | 1999 |
| 3 | Guide for Explosion and Bombing Scene Investigation | 8,033 | 2000 |
| 4 | Crime Scene Investigation: A Guide for Law Enforcement | 5,792 | 2000 |
| 5 | Understanding DNA Evidence: A Guide for Victim Service Providers | 5,343 | 2001 |
| 6 | Death Investigation: A Guide for the Scene Investigator | 4,930 | 1999 |
| 7 | Eyewitness Evidence: A Guide for Law Enforcement | 4,264 | 1999 |
| 8 | Fire and Arson Scene Evidence: A Guide for Public Safety Personnel | 3,406 | 2000 |
| 9 | Reducing Gun Violence: The Boston Gun Project's Operation Ceasefire | 2,869 | 2001 |
| 10 | Appropriate and Effective Use of Security Technologies in U.S. Schools | 2,040 | 1999 |
| 11 | Documenting Domestic Violence: How Health Care Providers Can Help Victims | 1,881 | 2001 |
| 12 | Mapping Crime: Principle and Practice | 1,863 | 1999 |
| 13 | Early Warning Systems: Responding to the Problem Officer | 1,739 | 2001 |
| 14 | National Institute of Justice Journal, Issue Number 248 | 1,721 | 2002 |
| 15 | Effects of Arrest on Intimate Partner Violence: New Evidence From the Spouse Assault Replication Program | 1,700 | 2001 |
| 16 | ADAM Preliminary Findings on Drug Use and Drug Markets: Adult Male Arrestees | 1,609 | 2000 |
| 17 | Privacy in the Information Age: A Guide for Sharing Crime Maps and Spatial Data | 1,576 | 2001 |
| 18 | Resource Guide to Law Enforcement, Corrections, and Forensic Technologies | 1,528 | 2001 |
| 19 | Protective Intelligence and Threat Assessment Investigations: A Guide for State and Local Law Enforcement Officials | 1,464 | 1998 |
| 20 | Policing on American Indian Reservations | 1,400 | 2001 |

TOP 20 NIJ PUBLICATIONS BY NUMBER OF ELECTRONIC COPIES ACCESSED FROM THE WEB, FY 2002

| | Hits | Title | URL | Year of Publication |
|---|---|---|---|---|
| 1 | 88,883 | Electronic Crime Scene Investigation: A Guide for First Responders | http://www.ncjrs.org/pdffiles1/nij/187736.pdf | 2001 |
| 2 | 61,215 | The Sexual Victimization of College Women | http://www.ncjrs.org/pdffiles1/nij/182369.pdf | 2000 |
| 3 | 56,273 | Crime Scene Investigation: A Guide for Law Enforcement | http://www.ncjrs.org/pdffiles1/nij/178280.pdf | 2000 |
| 4 | 53,761 | A Method to Assess the Vulnerability of U.S. Chemical Facilities | http://www.ncjrs.org/pdffiles1/nij/195171.pdf | 2002 |
| 5 | 52,127 | Extent, Nature, and Consequences of Intimate Partner Violence: Findings From the National Violence Against Women Survey | http://www.ncjrs.org/pdffiles1/nij/181867.pdf | 2000 |
| 6 | 48,489 | Guide for the Selection of Chemical Agent and Toxic Industrial Material Detection Equipment for Emergency First Responders, NIJ Guide 100–00, Volume 1 | http://www.ncjrs.org/pdffiles1/nij/184449.pdf | 2000 |
| 7 | 47,967 | Eyewitness Evidence: A Guide for Law Enforcement | http://www.ncjrs.org/pdffiles1/nij/178240.pdf | 1999 |
| 8 | 43,526 | Full Report of the Prevalence, Incidence, and Consequences of Violence Against Women: Findings From the National Violence Against Women Survey | http://www.ncjrs.org/pdffiles1/nij/183781.pdf | 2000 |
| 9 | 42,661 | An Introduction to Biological Agent Detection Equipment for Emergency First Responders, NIJ Guide 101–00 | http://www.ncjrs.org/pdffiles1/nij/190747.pdf | 2001 |
| 10 | 35,681 | Death Investigation: A Guide for the Scene Investigator | http://www.ncjrs.org/pdffiles/167568.pdf | 1999 |
| 11 | 35,359 | Reducing Gun Violence: The Boston Gun Project's Operation Ceasefire | http://www.ncjrs.org/pdffiles1/nij/188741.pdf | 2001 |
| 12 | 33,042 | Guide for the Selection of Chemical Agent and Toxic Industrial Material Detection Equipment for Emergency First Responders, NIJ Guide 100–00, Volume 2 | http://www.ncjrs.org/pdffiles1/nij/184450.pdf | 2000 |
| 13 | 31,006 | Use of Force By Police: Overview of National and Local Data | http://www.ncjrs.org/pdffiles1/nij/176330-1.pdf | 1999 |
| 14 | 30,276 | Selection and Application Guide to Personal Body Armor, NIJ Guide 100–01 | http://www.ncjrs.org/pdffiles1/nij/189633.pdf | 2001 |
| 15 | 28,458 | Preventing Crime: What Works, What Doesn't, What's Promising | http://www.ncjrs.org/works/wholedoc.htm | 1998 |
| 16 | 27,167 | A Resource Guide to Law Enforcement, Corrections, and Forensic Technologies | http://www.ncjrs.org/pdffiles1/nij/186822.pdf | 2001 |
| 17 | 24,916 | Mapping Crime: Principle and Practice | http://www.ncjrs.org/pdffiles1/nij/178919.pdf | 1999 |
| 18 | 24,543 | The Future of Forensic DNA Testing: Predictions of the Research and Development Working Group | http://www.ncjrs.org/pdffiles1/nij/183697.pdf | 2000 |
| 19 | 23,862 | Prevalence, Incidence, and Consequences of Violence Against Women: Findings From the National Violence Against Women Survey | http://www.ncjrs.org/pdffiles/172837.pdf | 1998 |
| 20 | 23,796 | Guide for the Selection of Communication Equipment for Emergency First Responders, NIJ Guide 104–00, Volume 1 | http://www.ncjrs.org/pdffiles1/nij/191160.pdf | 2002 |

APPENDIX D
# Web Site Statistics in FY 2002

NUMBER OF VISITS TO NIJ WEB SITE, BY MONTH,*

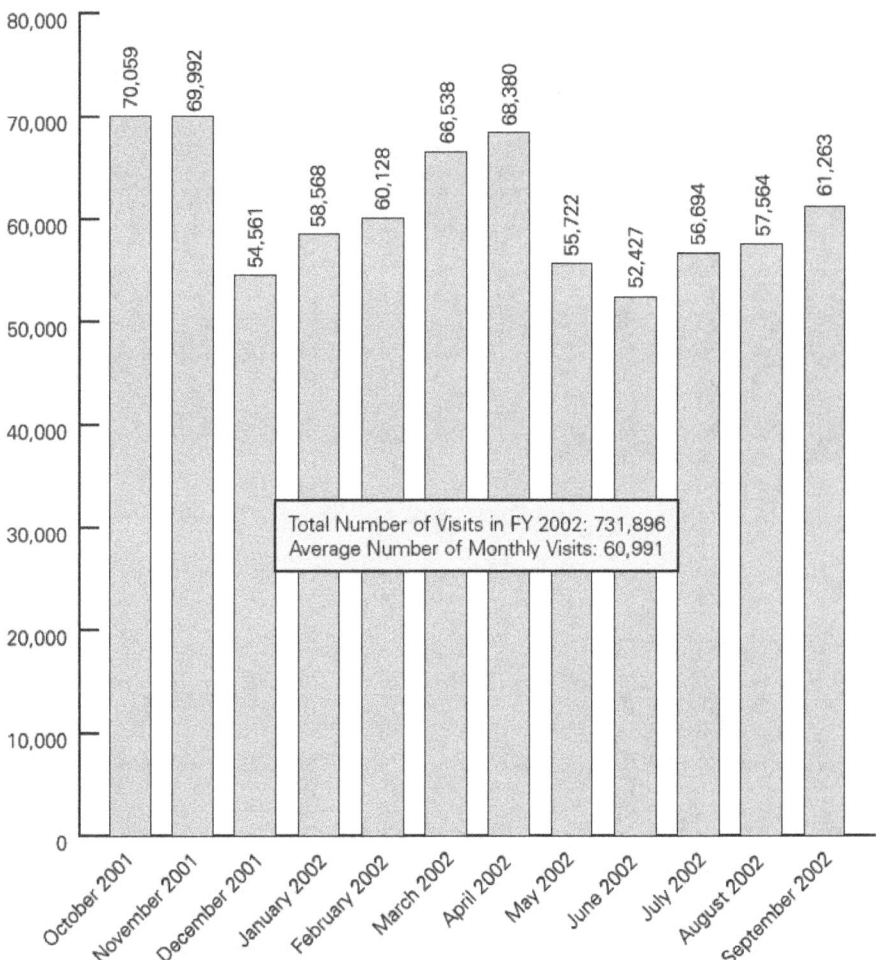

Total Number of Visits in FY 2002: 731,896
Average Number of Monthly Visits: 60,991

*A "visit" begins when a visitor views the first NIJ Web page and ends when the visitor leaves the NIJ site or remains idle beyond 30 minutes.

APPENDIX E
# Key Conferences

**Sixth Annual Mock Prison Riot,** former West Virginia Penitentiary in Moundsville, May 5–9, 2002, West Virginia. 1,235 attended, representing 33 States and 5 countries.

**Third Annual DNA Grantees Workshop,** June 24–26, 2002, Washington, DC. 223 attended.

**Annual Conference on Criminal Justice Research and Evaluation,** "Enhancing Policy and Practice," July 21–24, 2002, Washington, D.C. 820 attended.

**Fourth National Conference on Science and the Law,** October 3–5, 2002, Miami, Florida. 140 attended.

**Sixth Annual International Crime Mapping Research Conference: Bridging the Gap Between Research and Practice,** December 8–11, 2002, Denver, Colorado. 323 attended, including 48 international visitors representing 17 countries.

The National Institute of Justice is the research, development, and evaluation agency of the U.S. Department of Justice. NIJ provides objective, independent, evidence-based knowledge and tools to enhance the administration of justice and public safety.

The National Institute of Justice is a component of the Office of Justice Programs, which also includes the Bureau of Justice Assistance, the Bureau of Justice Statistics, the Office of Juvenile Justice and Delinquency Prevention, and the Office for Victims of Crime.

*Photo Sources: Brand X Pictures, Comstock Images, and Getty Images.*

NCJ 200338

www.ingramcontent.com/pod-product-compliance
Lightning Source LLC
Chambersburg PA
CBHW070511290526
45790CB00003B/1187

* 9 7 8 1 5 0 2 7 9 9 9 0 6 *